Primer

Joel O'Brien

Presentation by *BookLeaf Publishing*

Web: www.bookleafpub.com

E-mail: info@bookleafpub.com

ISBN: 9789358319187

First edition 2023

My Favorite Childhood Memory

It was the day after Easter, a Monday.
I was 4.
I was playing in the front yard, eating my
chocolate bunny.
The neighborhood bully came by on his bike
& said "You don't need all that" and took it
away.

After dinner I was in the front yard with my
sister when he rode by again.
The hero of our story grabbed a stick,
Chased his bike down ON FOOT
Put her stick into the spokes of his front tire,
Sent him flying off of his bike,
& told him to stay away from her brother.
It was a very good day in Zemple,

Kmart Cafe

When was about three, my grandparents had a
rather volatile divorce.
When I was four, my grandma married his
second wife. No surprise. Volatile divorces are
often followed by a rather quick remarriage.
The day of the wedding, I went to Kmart with
my mom and my aunt.
I excitedly approached the cafe to order an Icee,
as any normal child at Kmart in the '80s would.
I don't remember if I ordered blue, red, or cola
that day. I don't even remember if I ordered an
Icee at all.
I do however remember opening my mouth to
order, but as if I was a fortune telling toddler
reporting on the impending marriage, I threw up.
My mom must've really needed whatever we
went there for, because we went about our
shopping instead of leaving in a cloud of
humiliation.

Moccasins and a Homemade Afghan

I don't really know when I became aware of Dolly Parton. I do know that her first song that I followed the release of was her 1991 hit "Eagle When She Flies". She released a lot of good songs during that period, starred in the hit (in my head) movie "Straight Talk", and often had the closing number on award shows. Dolly was hot! It was also during this time that if someone would have come home quietly at just the right time, they could have caught me wrapped in a '70s afghan with moccasins upon my feet as I belted out "Jolene".

The Year We Became a Fake Tree Family

I grew up hating going out in the woods to get a Christmas tree. Northern Minnesota is cold in December. It's even colder when your parents never like the same tree. I would beg for a fake tree.

One year, our dog Allie had to be put to sleep a few days after Thanksgiving. As we were driving home with the corpse of our dog in the trunk of the car to be buried in the yard, my dad announced we were stopping at Kmart for a fake tree since I'd been wanting one. This was my year!

While I stayed out in the car with Allie's recently departed vessel, my mom and dad finally picked out our first tree that everyone loved.

Field of the Millennia

5

It seems like yesterday
But sometimes so long ago that it was someone
else
Dreaming about all of the people, places, and
things
That would cease to exist
If what they said was true

She Was Not Expecting That

A few years ago, I had to have my very first dog that I got as an adult, and was only mine, put to sleep.
The day before we were sending him off, I carried him to the park a couple blocks away a few times to go to the bathroom. As I was waiting to cross the street, a lady told me that I had a wonderful dog.
Not only did I start sobbing, but we both walked the same direction for an awkward block and a half.
I wish I had noticed her reaction, because it makes me laugh now. Can you imagine complementing someone and having them start sobbing?

Dating Apps & Tattoos

On a trip to LA with my then boyfriend, we got matching tattoos. Thankfully, they were simple line drawings so when I was unceremoniously dumped, I planned to go get it colored in or something so we wouldn't match anymore.
I've never gotten around to doing it, because awhile back I saw him on a dating app.
Not only did he lose five years off his age and grow a penis in his mouth, but he colored in his tattoo.

You're Not A Plant Dad

Part of the reason I'm single is because I'm a lot pickier than someone with a wonky eye should maybe be. I don't care. You're not a plant dad. Stop making up words and stick to posting pictures of your dick next to your cable TV remote so I can try to figure out if you're rich enough to afford cable or just really bad with money.

How Bad Can It Be?

I used to have neighbors that would occasionally have loud drunk domestic arguments in the middle of the night. It really irritated me. If you have to be drunk to have your loud fight, your problems can't be that bad. Get over yourself and count your blessings.
I couldn't believe their nerve when I saw them staring at us as we tried out for the Springer show in the front yard at 11am. Sober. Those are real problems.
If you have to be drunk in the middle of the night to put on a show for the neighbors, your problem is alcohol, not each other.

Dear Fuckface,

I just had a long day at work and I'm just trying
to get home. Who in the hell do you think you
are to drive like that?
I'm listening to my Jesus music (with one free
ear) and crossing on a walk light in the
crosswalk.
My mood is good. I'm done working for the day.
I'm probably about to try to hit this high note
with Cece.
You come barreling into the crosswalk,
sometimes fucking about on your phone,
sometimes just being an entitled fuck. Always
coming right up on me.
So anyways, I just wanted to let you know why I
called you that seventeen syllable word. My
mother certainly taught me better. She would
have done it in four.

Scooters & Gate Doors

Citizens,

I'm going to need you to stop leaving those stupid rental bikes and scooters on the middle of the sidewalk. Also, stop blasting down the sidewalk on your scooters. You're stupid and rude.

If you have a fence with a gate, close it. Too many of you are leaving the gate open. It then opens, blocking the public sidewalk. Someday, I am going to superglue your gates closed since you are also stupid and rude.

The city sidewalks are already an obstacle course due to the fun combo of them all being completely uneven, and the lack of streetlights. Thank you.

1st World Problems Are Legitimate & Other Homemaking Tips

Have you ever needed a gift card for someone but the store was opening late that day? Have you ever had to crawl into a weeping willow because there wasn't a public bathroom anywhere for most of 2020? Did your take out burrito bowl leak juices into the paper bag? Your issues are certainly problems for you, but don't wallow. It makes you sound ungrateful.

Buy the gift card online. You don't have to go to a store for that anymore. Be grateful you had a weeping willow to pee in. It probably was more luxurious than a port a potty. Bring a plastic bag (that you'll reuse later for a garbage bag or dog poop bag) to carry your brown paper bag full of burrito both home in. The bag won't rip, and you won't get juices on your clothes.

Visiting Hours

I like reading the jail roster from the county
where I grew up.
I feel some empathy and maybe even pray for
the nice people who just never seem to get their
footing in life.

I get great pleasure, way too much pleasure,
when I see the mugshots of my enemies.
Dressed in the bright orange jumpsuit, with a
faded pink t-shirt underneath, looking so much
older than I do.

Recently, I cast my eyes upon the face of the one
who threw a snowball at my face. I got a lot of
enjoyment from that.

A week or two later, his father was listed right
underneath his listing. I was filled with a loving
glow as I thought how sweet it was that they
would get to spend some time together. When I
was in jail, my dad just came for a half hour
visiting block.

Communion

Red wine is disgusting. It smells like compost. Grape juice is not my favorite either. Jesus knows of my aversion and the reason why, so I can't help but think He would be ok with me substituting grape Waterloo, or even some Diet Coke.

Let Go & Let God

At this point in my life, I do not recommend revenge. I suppose I figure it's usually morally wrong. It's OK to fantasize a little, if it doesn't interfere with reality.

I've outlived a double crosser or two, some are in jail or prison, some have funny looking kids, and some have just aged bably.

I had nothing to do with any of that. I didn't have to do a thing, but victory is mine!

1983

It's a real shithole
Houses are even haunted
Don't swim in the lake

There aren't any stores
Do you want to pee outside
Let's go get gumballs

Window

Do you have some Windex
And maybe some paper towel
Preferably not the cheap kind
You just use more
I have to clean my window
I think I have a blind spot
Do you?

Sister Mister

Sister keep your voice down sister
Mister keep your voice down mister
It's 6 in the morning, still dark outside
Nobody wants to be on this ride.

The Legend of Felonious Junk

Once upon a time & not so long ago
Just over a couple of streets
Was a man who could blow the sax
And make everybody dance
But it just didn't pay the bills
With no health insurance and children needing
pills
So he put on a penis costume & he went outside
And then he robbed everyone who laughed at
him
And that was that.
And that's the Legend of Felonious Junk